Crocus

A Photo Essay

by

Stephen M Kraemer

© 2019 Stephen M. Kraemer

Originality

Winter Light

Palettes

Enchanted Hours

Regalia

Sesquicentennial

Collaboration

Standout

Nature's Way

Lightning

Temptation

Orchestral

Reflectivity

Golden Rainbow

Reductions

Softer Tones

Perplexed

Lit up

Medallion

www.ingramcontent.com/pod-product-compliance
Lightning Source LLC
Chambersburg PA
CBHW041115180526
45172CB00001B/254